School-University Collaboration

by
Karen A. Verbeke
and
Patricia O. Richards

ISBN 0-87367-685-8
Copyright © 2001 by the Phi Delta Kappa Educational Foundation
Bloomington, Indiana

This fastback is sponsored by the
Northern Illinois University Chapter
of Phi Delta Kappa International,
which made a generous contribution
toward publication costs.

The chapter sponsors this fastback
to honor Jim and Jan Byrne,
recently retired secondary school
English teachers in St. Charles and
Geneva, Illinois. The Byrnes each
have served the chapter faithfully
as president and in
numerous other chapter offices.

Table of Contents

Introduction

School and university partnerships have existed for more than a century. However, the purpose of most of these collaborations has been locating field placements for preservice teachers, conducting research, and providing inservice workshops. There was little interest in overall school improvement, and the two institutions lacked a common goal (Cook and Friend 1991; Pugach and Johnson 1995).

Within the past two decades, the relationship has changed. Collaboration now presents a real opportunity to make systemic change and improvement, true education reform. However, collaboration is complex, challenging, and synergistic. For many schools and universities, this can be daunting.

The individuals involved in any collaboration can make it even more complicated. Each person involved will have his or her own perspective on the process and the goals to be accomplished. In addition, each person also will reflect the specific agenda of the institution he or she represents. Thus one of the first tasks of any collaboration is to build understanding and consensus among diverse stakeholders. Understanding the values and orientation of each stakeholder is important; it is the foundation for mutual respect. And it is out of that respect that groups can begin to shape a shared vision and purpose.

Each organization involved in a collaborative effort will have its own mission. These institutional missions need to be shared early in the process in order for the stakeholders to create a new shared vision for their initiative. If the missions and visions of the organizations involved are deemed incompatible, then collaboration cannot succeed.

In addition to institutional missions, collaborators need to be aware of agendas — the explicit or implicit goals of the stakeholders. Agendas can be hidden or overt, mandated or voluntary, external or internal. To the degree possible, they must be presented, understood, and clarified at the beginning of the process. Often, it is the hidden, political agenda that emerges later. When someone stumbles on it, sometimes in an unsuspecting way, it can wreak havoc.

Collaboration also requires a commitment in the form of time and resources, which need to be identified early in the process. These commitments can be increased when the goals of the collaborative effort are complex. Multifaceted collaborative projects with multiple goals and several different groups of stakeholders create additional challenges to the process.

Factors Influencing Success or Failure

The reason for starting a collaboration often determines the degree to which the initiative is successful. Mandated collaborations often require much more time and additional resources. In contrast, when collaboration is based on mutual need, there usually is a sense of urgency that creates high motivation for all stakeholders to work together in a timely way with fewer resources.

Perhaps the most important factor determining the success of a collaboration is a willingness of the various stakeholders to collaborate. Coerced collaboration may sound like an unlikely possibility, but it is becoming quite common.

Regulatory agencies and accrediting organizations are requiring universities with teacher preparation programs to partner with K-12 schools in the creation of professional development schools (Wise and Lubbrand 1996). The professional development school (PDS) combines the traditional K-12 and university collaboration of placing student teachers with experienced K-12 teachers and the once-prevalent university laboratory schools, which provided for long-term internship opportunities and demonstration teaching. Added to that mix is the professional development of inservice teachers and university faculty. Theoretically, experienced teachers and student teachers both develop professionally through a closer relationship with each other. University faculty, in turn, benefit from more time spent in K-12 classrooms. The PDS concept strives to bridge the divide between the ivory tower and the real world.

While the terms "K-16 collaboration" and "professional development schools" appear routinely in the literature on teacher preparation and school improvement, the long-term outcomes of these initiatives have yet to be assessed systematically.

Coerced collaboration is not an ideal way to begin a relationship. The metaphor of the shotgun wedding comes to mind. The participants are forced into a partnership with little choice. This certainly is an inhibiting factor because no one enjoys being told what to do.

However, a coerced collaboration may, on occasion, benefit both parties. As is the case in some arranged marriages, the partnership may work to everyone's satisfaction with desirable benefits for all.

An example of this unusual situation is the collaboration between the University of Maryland Eastern Shore (UMES) and Salisbury University (SU). If K-12 and university collaboration is uncommon, collaboration between higher education institutions is even more so, particularly for two such different institutions as UMES and SU. Founded in 1886, UMES is a historically black university, while SU was founded in 1925 as a two-year state teachers college. The missions of both institutions have expanded over the years. Though only 12 miles away from each other, the traditional relationship of the two universities was competitive. In 1988, both universities became sister institutions when the Maryland legislature created the University System of Maryland (USM) under a single board of regents, who discouraged competitiveness and program duplication. There was talk of merging the two institutions into one comprehensive university. Collaborative agreements on program offerings and dual-degree programs were the best chance for both universities to retain their individuality, vital programs, and resources (Nnadi et al. 2000). Without the mandate in 1988, it is unlikely that either university would have survived the financial hard times experienced by Maryland's higher education institutions in the early 1990s, when many colleges were required to discontinue programs because of limited resources. The two institutions have been able to retain most of the programs originally slated for elimination and have been able to share resources and attract additional resources to develop new programs due to their creative partnership. This collaboration continues today.

The edict to "collaborate or perish" was a powerful motivator, but it was not the reason for the success of this particular collaboration. In fact, there were a series of meetings among groups within the universities, and they discovered and developed common goals. There also were people who knew one another from their associations outside of their workplaces, and people were willing to take risks in an attempt to get beyond their institutional histories and baggage. One powerful incentive was the chance to retain or increase resources for programs that administrators, faculty, students, and the communities held dear. This gave the partners a shared goal, perhaps the most essential factor among all those that can make a collaboration a success. The individual and shared benefits of the collaboration are what have kept the process alive and made it worth the constant effort needed to maintain a productive, ongoing relationship.

Coerced collaboration does not always work out so well. Making the best out of a bad situation is not the optimal note on which to begin a collaborative process. Trust flourishes when participants willingly enter into collaborative relationships. It develops more rapidly when participants can select the partners with whom they wish to collaborate. Mutual trust fosters risk taking, experimentation, and growth. It occurs over time and cannot be forced.

In voluntary collaborations, who makes the decision to collaborate plays an important role in the success or failure of the venture. The level at which the decision is made reveals a great deal about the goals of the collaboration and institutional commitment to those goals.

Often, upper-level administrators make the determination to enter into a collaborative agreement. Faculty may not have been part of the decision-making process at either the school or university level. University deans and school superintendents may initiate collaborative agreements without input or assent from those who ultimately will be responsible for implementing the initiative. Their purpose may be to secure grant funding or to enhance their institutional images with policy makers or the community. These administrators are not likely to be the ones carrying out the day-to-day activities of the collaborative endeavor. Like coerced collaboration, the outcomes of these "voluntary" top-down arrangements are questionable. The initiatives may manage to meet minimal expectations of the arrangement, but greater results are doubtful.

Conversely, collaborative agreements may be made at the school and university faculty level without the involvement of higher administrators. This creates problems related to resources, performance evaluation, and the life span of the collaboration. The agreement can be terminated unilaterally by those at a higher decision-making level at any time. The original intent of the collaborative initiative also may be jeopardized if the ultimate power brokers — who generally are not faculty — may be unwilling to support goals that they do not perceive as a priority.

Decisions about changes in personnel can end a collaboration. Collaborative agreements often are the brain child of a few individuals. Sometimes the collaboration is completely dependent on a few individuals. For example, a productive, two-year collaboration in the form of a PDS came to a screeching halt when the school principal was involuntarily transferred, because of outstanding performance, to another school. The new principal was inexperienced and unwilling to continue the PDS.

Mandates from policy makers above the collaborative level can threaten collaboration. The K-12 schools often do not have final decision-making authority. State departments of education and federal regulations often impose requirements that constrain or disrupt the collaboration's goals. High-stakes assessments, prescriptive school-wide reform programs, and phonics-first legislation are some examples of this phenomenon. Consider a newly-initiated PDS collaboration between an elementary school and a university with a highly regarded teacher preparation program. The collaboration was initiated by the partners for the expressed purposes of providing long-term experiences for teacher candidates in challenging elementary school classrooms and for improving K-6 reading achievement through university faculty assistance and expertise. The nascent collaboration is derailed when, under threat of reconstitution, the elementary school adopts a prescribed curriculum at the behest of the state department of education. Because there are many effective approaches to teaching reading, it would be unconscionable for a university to consider a school that adopts a scripted, one-size-fits-all program as a professional development school. The elementary school teachers are no longer professionals who are expected to expand their repertoires and knowledge of effective instructional practices. They merely deliver the program as prescribed. The university faculty members in the PDS no longer have a role to play or a contribution to make. End of collaboration.

Collaboration is affected by many other factors. Each factor's influences on the collaboration depend on the unique attributes of the particular situation. Each of these factors can have a profound effect. In some cases, a particular factor might undermine the collaborative process entirely; in other cases, it might result in an unanticipated success. Therefore, they merit serious thought and open discussion.

In addition to the willingness to collaborate, the factors are: shared goals; institutional cultural differences including mission, organizational structure, rewards, professional development, and autonomy; assessment and accountability; such individual cultural differences as professional status, socioeconomic status, age, gender, race, ethnicity, and sexual orientation; and communication, including written agreements specifying time, resources, roles, responsibilities, decision making, goals, process assessment, and outcomes evaluation.

Shared Goals

The importance of agreeing on goals, clearly expressed and equally valued by all, cannot be overstated. Shared goals are critical to a successful collaboration. Shared goals make it possible for a collaboration to succeed, even under adverse conditions and unlikely pairings, as evidenced in the case of University of Maryland Eastern Shore and Salisbury University. The lack of shared goals significantly inhibits the collaborative process.

It would seem logical that collaborative partners would not enter into a collaborative arrangement unless they did have shared goals, except, perhaps, in the case of coerced collaborations. Even then, one would assume that some shared goal was apparent to the initiating party. Unfortunately, that is not always the case. Goals often are expressed in broad terms, thus leaving them open to various interpretations. The desired outcomes may not be clearly defined. And collaborative partners may share common long-term goals, but their short-term goals may not be similar.

In addition, "way finding" often occurs in the achievement of goals, both in the short and long term. Way finding describes the alternate routes taken by individuals in pursuit of a common outcome or objective. There are many routes to the same destination, and a disagreement about the route can be divisive, even though there may be no disagreement as to the destination. Moreover, goals may appear to be similar and shared when they are not.

For example, at first glance, K-12 institutions and teacher preparation programs appear to have common goals; and they do, to some extent. Both are concerned with providing quality education in a democratic society. But while a K-12 inservice teacher may supervise a student teacher, that teacher places the goal of future teacher preparation at a much lower priority than the goal of achievement for her or his own K-12 students. Conversely, the university supervisor is more concerned with the success of the preservice teacher, the university supervisor's own student, than with the achievement of the K-l 2 students or the professional development of the K-12 teacher.

The long-term goal of a quality education for all students may exist at the national and state level as a common goal.

The PDS is perceived as the way to accomplish this goal by policy makers. In reality, it is not a goal easily accomplished by the university and K-12 participants in the short term, in the same way, or to the same extent. Higher education institutions and K-12 schools are different organizations with different missions and, therefore, different goals.

Increasing K-12 student achievement is not the primary goal of university teacher preparation programs. Improving teacher preparation programs is not the primary goal of K-12 schools; improving achievement of K-12 students is their goal. The time regular teachers spend on mentoring preservice interns and collaborating with university faculty is time diverted from working directly with K-12 students.

The PDS concept initially appears to be a logical one based on the goals shared by all participants, but it is not quite so straightforward when the collaborating partners' clearly and specifically articulated goals are considered. That is not to say that common goals can not be developed and shared between K-12 schools and teacher preparation programs, but it does mean a successful collaboration requires more than the perception of long-term goals held in common.

Institutional Differences

Higher education institutions and K-12 schools are distinctively different entities. These institutions have very different missions, organizational structures, reward systems, and perceptions of faculty development and autonomy. In addition, within these institutions, administrators, teachers, support staffs, students, and parents, among others, may each perceive and participate in a different subculture or set of subcultures (Sternberg 2000).

Sternberg characterizes education institutions as organisms with a life of their own. He cautions that failure to recognize their organic properties dooms attempts at change. The whole is greater than the sum its parts because of the complex interactions among these parts (2000, p. 8). Therefore, when two separate and distinct "organisms" attempt to join forces, that complexity of interactions increases exponentially. The differences in organizational cultures and subcultures exert considerable influence on collaborative ventures.

Mission. Ostensibly K-12 schools exist to provide an education to all students in order to prepare citizens for full participation in a democratic society. Higher education institutions, at the undergraduate level, select their students and then strive to educate them in the arts and sciences. In addition, they prepare undergraduates for careers or for graduate study. Universities, public and private, can determine the criteria for accepting and retaining students; public K-12 schools cannot. In order to accomplish their respective missions, K-12 schools and higher education institutions are organized in different ways with dissimilar governance policies and procedures. Time and tradition have shaped these institutions, rooting them in organizational structures resistant to change.

Organizational Structures. Organizations have different governance structures for making decisions. While all organizations have designated lines of authority, universities have more decentralized decision-making structures than those in K-12 institutions. University faculty are used to more autonomy and more decision-making authority than are K-12 faculty. In the university, faculty have considerable control over curriculum, materials, and pedagogy. Decisions in these areas routinely are made at the department level. In K-12 schools, individual faculty members have little decision-making authority. School improvement teams comprising faculty members and building-level administrators may develop plans, but those plans must be approved at the district level. Because it is more decentralized and participative, university decision making is also more deliberative. Decisions are not made as quickly as they are in centralized organizations. The differences in governance may cause confusion and frustration on the part of school and university partners unless their respective organizational structures and procedures are made apparent to each other.

Reward Systems. The performance criteria for K-12 faculty and university faculty differ significantly. The primary evaluation of K-12 faculty is based on satisfactory classroom teaching, as determined by a principal and possibly a central office administrator. University faculty are evaluated on the basis of teaching, scholarship, service to the university, and service to the community. Faculty must provide evidence of successful teaching, which usually comes in the form of student evaluations, department chairperson evaluations, and peer evaluations. Even at universities whose mission is primarily teaching, rather than research, teaching constitutes approximately 60% to 75% of faculty members' professional time. Scholarly activities and service, in the form of committee membership at the department, school, and university level, are required. Working in collaborative arrangements at K-12 schools may be considered teaching only when the faculty member is supervising university interns, thereby generating credit hours.

This difference in job criteria and reward structures creates real tension for university faculty. Collaborative endeavors that require the university faculty member to be at the K-12 school for planning and meetings, in addition to on-site "teaching" responsibilities, can hamper the faculty member's ability to engage in traditional scholarship and can reduce his or her participation on university committees.

One model that may ameliorate this problem has been suggested by Boyer in *Scholarship Reconsidered* (1990). But it can help this problem only to the extent that his model is accepted by the university as tenure and promotion criteria. Even then, time spent at K-12 schools is time spent away from campus. It is very much like having two jobs with two offices, two teaching venues, and two sets of colleagues. Giving adequate time to both becomes a serious challenge.

Another solution may be for universities to hire clinical faculty, faculty members whose primary responsibilities are fulfilled off campus at the collaborative site. These faculty members would be evaluated differently than regular faculty and would be exempt from the requirements of traditional scholarship, service on university committees, and student advising. However, care must be taken so that clinical faculty do not have lower status than non-clinical university faculty.

Reward structures and evaluation criteria play a powerful role in collaboration. Without significant systemic change in traditional reward structures, school-university collaborations will be seriously impeded. Maeroff indicates that while school-university collaborative attempts have proliferated, their effect remains limited, hampered principally by policies at universities that do not reward and may even penalize faculty members who involve themselves with elementary and secondary schools (2000, p. 34).

The K-12 faculty is not exempt from the problems caused by traditional reward structures. If classroom teaching effectiveness is measured only by student achievement, a K-12 teacher may understandably be reluctant to engage in collaborative endeavors that divert time and energy away from students. In addition, parents and school board members may object to K-12 faculty spending time on anything that does not involve direct student contact and may object to experimentation and to preservice interns working with K-12 students. This is especially likely in very high-achieving schools, where there is pressure to maintain high performance, and in very low-achieving schools, where there is pressure to increase student achievement, often through uniform curricula and prescribed pedagogy.

Professional Development and Faculty Autonomy. Professional development is viewed very differently in K-12 and university settings. The one-size-fits-all model has been and remains the prevailing model of K-12 faculty development. Administrators evaluate faculty and make determinations about the faculty's professional needs. Everyone gets the same thing because conformity is easier to manage than diversity, thereby giving it value in a centralized organization. Also, K-12 faculty are accustomed to professional development occurring in the form of traditional university courses because certification requires the continuation of formal education through graduate study. Both K-12 administrators and teachers have been enculturated in a manner that leaves them looking to "experts," rather than peers or themselves, for professional development.

While there has been a movement away from this model toward a more individualized approach to faculty development, it is still in its infancy. Individualized plans for faculty development are challenging to create, administer, and evaluate. So while some experimentation with this model exists, K-12 faculty development still is delivered much as it has always been.

Cost effectiveness and time efficiency are major advantages of the traditional model, even though the results of this type of faculty development are exceedingly questionable. These factors, combined with the persistent perception of K-12 faculty as only an instrument of curriculum delivery and the growing movement toward the deprofessionalization of teachers, make change very difficult.

The decentralized structure of universities supports the notion of individual professional development. University faculty development is considered to occur through one's scholarship, and each faculty member's scholarship is determined by the faculty member's area of expertise and research interests. One-size-fits-all models of faculty development at universities are rare and exceedingly ill received. University faculty are vocal and protective about their rights in this regard. University faculty are often accorded the status of professionals and treated as such.

Research is valued differently by university faculty and K-12 faculty. Traditionally, K-12 faculty have not viewed research as useful or practical. It is not something they routinely read, nor do they engage regularly in conducting research. Conversely, university faculty value research and willingly engage not only in conducting research, but also in responding to it by testing it, interpreting it, applying it, or refuting it. They view research as a primary means of professional development. Individual research interests and differences in philosophies are the norm in higher education. Skepticism and debate abound, and compromise is less frequent than are agreements to disagree.

Universities are less likely to embrace curricular trends or pedagogical fads because university faculty generally enjoy more authority than do K-12 faculty. Institutional change occurs much more slowly and deliberately and is less likely to be imposed by administrators. There is more tolerance for diverse views and approaches because higher education institutions are expected to promote critical thinking and individual decision making.

The university general education curriculum emphasizes the arts and sciences, which themselves are composed of many disciplines with various modes of inquiry and communication. The K-12 curriculum tends to be narrower in scope and hierarchical in sequence. Major curricular decisions in schools are made at the central office level, not at the classroom level or the school level. The search for the one best program or method is prevalent and not surprising in an organization where decision making is centralized and where there is the expectation that students will receive a comparable education from school to school. Faculty are viewed as the means of delivering the curriculum, not developing the curriculum. The standards movement and the rising popularity of schoolwide improvement programs are testaments to this way of thinking about K-12 faculty.

Assessment and Accountability

Philosophies and practices related to assessment and accountability constitute another cultural difference between schools and universities. Accountability for student achievement in schools is considered a faculty responsibility as much as, or more than, an individual student responsibility. In a university, accountability for student achievement rests with the individual student. University faculty are not taxed with the same degree of responsibility as are K-12 faculty because the institutional mission is fundamentally different, as is the student population.

External assessment prevails in K-12 schools. Schools must demonstrate student achievement in order to qualify for federal and state funding and to satisfy the public, who finances the school system. Top-down evaluation prevails, with criterion- or norm-referenced, standardized tests as the instruments of choice so that population comparisons can be made within and across districts and states.

Universities are less accustomed to such prescribed external evaluation. Typically they are not required by licensing agencies to evaluate overall student achievement by means of criterion- or norm-referenced tests. Higher education institutions are accountable to boards of regents and accrediting organizations, but self-studies are used to present evidence of the accomplishment of the university's mission. Higher education institutions have more input in developing criteria for making determinations about institutional effectiveness and have more latitude in how they present evidence.

As mentioned in the discussion of reward structures, K-12 faculty are used to being evaluated externally, whereas university faculty are accustomed to self-assessment. However, higher education faculty have become increasingly alarmed as the accountability movement gains momentum and spills over from K-12 schools into initial teacher preparation programs. For example, standardized tests now are required for teacher certification. In addition, Title II legislation now mandates that higher education institutions with teacher preparation programs report the Praxis scores of their teacher candidates, thus making the universities more publicly accountable for their students' performance. Federal funding will be tied to compliance with this mandate. This now becomes a high-stakes venture for higher education institutions in much the same way as statewide testing is for K-12 schools. Failure to attain passing scores on the examination means that, despite a degree from an accredited university, one cannot be certified to teach. Federal funding would be denied to low-performing higher education institutions. Yet, while higher education faculty may now be more sympathetic to accountability pressures placed on K-12 faculty, there remain essential differences between how assessment is viewed and implemented in K-12 schools and higher education institutions.

The issues of assessment and accountability are complicated, at best, in any situation. But in school-university collaborations, there is a temptation to avoid raising these issues. However, assessment is essential in collaborative agreements. Enduring gains result from well-defined, clearly articulated goals and evaluation measures to gauge the achievement of those goals. Assessment should not be only a summation of what the collaboration has produced, but also a formative mechanism for improving the collaboration process (Maeroff 2000).

There are important, difficult questions that must be addressed. How does one measure progress in a process? How does one assess dispositions and attitudes? How does one assess individual stakeholders' commitment to the collaboration? What evidence best demonstrates the accomplishment of the goals? How can it be gathered and presented efficiently?

Individual Differences

Another constraining aspect of school-university collaboration is that of the diversity of the stakeholders as individuals. The slogan about diversity being the spice of life fails to take into account the unpleasant effects created by an unharmonious mixture of spices. Diversity cannot be treated in simplistic terms. Individuals are the most complex component in collaboration.

The school-university collaboration requires individuals to work cooperatively with individuals they do not normally work with. The roles they have in their respective institutional hierarchies may be altered, according more status to some and diminishing the autonomy and authority of others. The new roles and relationships created by the collaboration need careful attention. Predictably, people's interactions will be heavily influenced by their current status and by past experiences. Regrettably, history has left us a troubled legacy with regard to professional status, socioeconomic status, age, gender, sexual orientation, race, and ethnicity.

Professional Status. Higher education faculty generally are accorded more status and respect as professionals than are K-12 faculty. Therefore a school-university collaboration may be perceived in terms of the K-12 faculty on the front lines with the university faculty planning the campaign strategies and preparing more troops, that is, more preservice interns. This assumption creates one dynamic if all of the collaborative participants willingly accept it, but it creates quite another dynamic if some of the participants do not.

Preservice interns may perceive K-12 faculty as more expert than university faculty in the K-12 environment. This lowers the status of the university supervisor and grants informal authority to the K-12 cooperating teacher, even though the supervisor may have formal authority over the preservice intern. How does this, in turn, influence the relationship of the university supervisor and cooperating teacher when they are working together toward mutual professional growth? In cases where the instructional practices of the cooperating teacher are effective, it may simply be a case of each needing to set aside ego and to work for the good of the cause. But it is a different situation entirely if effective instructional practices are not modeled by the cooperating teacher. Working for the good of the cause might now be a two-against-one proposition. In addition, setting ego aside is easier said than done.

Teachers tend to have a great deal of humility, may not view themselves as experts, and may be reticent to highlight their expertise when it very much exists. University faculty may be accorded more status, as well as informal authority, by K-12 faculty than that ceded to K-12 principals or curriculum supervisors. Higher education colleagues may be perceived as allies, whereas administrators may be perceived as adversaries.

Administrators in K-12 settings may find university faculty a bit uppity, overreaching what they view as appropriate authority roles of faculty based on the K-12 centralized structure. University faculty, used to exercising control over curriculum and instruction, may tend to operate outside the K-12 chain of command in a school-university collaboration. Alternatively, university faculty may align themselves more with administrators than with K-12 faculty because of the lower status accorded to K-12 faculty. Titles and levels of education attainment also may influence relationships.

In essence, the status quo no longer exists in a school-university collaborative initiative. Ideally, this should be a positive feature, permitting everyone's contributions to enrich the collaboration. Rank and status should be used for the accomplishment of the venture's goals. Moving flexibly between old roles and new ones in order to further the initiative is a goal worth achieving. It is best to realize this and to discuss new roles and relationships so that these factors do not inhibit a productive and peaceful union.

Individual Status. Historically, psychologists have identified and studied attributes of individuals. Maccoby (1990) indicates that on most psychological attributes, there is a wide variation among individuals. A major focus of research has been the effort to identify sources of this variation. Values, attitudes, and beliefs may be shaped by socioeconomlc status, age, gender, race, ethnicity, and sexual orientation; however, this shaping may not occur in predictable ways. Maccoby's point about wide variation among individuals must be noted. Stereotyping must be recognized and resisted.

Given the demographics, present and forecasted, the school-university collaboration undoubtedly will include an increasingly diverse mix of individuals. Special attention will need to be given to this vital aspect of the collaborative process.

Socioeconomic status (SES) is a familiar term in education. It influences a multitude of education factors, and it is invoked most often in reference to K-12 students. Publishers promote programs and materials for high-risk students, those with lower SES. Standardized tests favor those with a higher SES. Home-school programs take into account SES. Individuals' perceptions and interactions may be influenced by SES. This is just as true for school-university collaborative participants as for other groups.

Participants in a school-university collaboration need to be aware of their own assumptions based on their SES group. These assumptions may be unconscious and unexamined. The best solution is to raise this issue, creating awareness and inviting dialogue so that barriers to understanding are avoided. The conversations may be uncomfortable, but allowing discomfort to stifle them is a mistake.

Chronological age is another variable that may affect the relationships of individuals in a collaboration. Wisdom does not automatically come with age. Practice makes permanent, but not necessarily perfect. Those of a particular age have not all shared the same experiences. As a result, they may have come to different understandings about what constitutes effective practice. Conflicting ideas about what constitutes a quality education abound and always have. Thus it is dangerous to make assumptions based only on age and years of experience as to who the experts are and whose opinions should carry the most weight.

Guided inquiry of the professional literature on effective practices would be a useful activity early in the collaborative initiative. Multi-age study groups are recommended to help participants engage in informed dialogue about best practices and identify points of agreement among researchers and themselves. Study groups promote the idea of learning together. Using professional literature for guided inquiry in regard to best practice identifies traditional and contemporary approaches, thus bridging the age gap. It reduces the risk of individuals using years of service as a status device or as an indication of degree of expertise.

Much has been written on gender differences. Differences in communication styles have been noted between men and women, as have differences in their behavior while in groups performing tasks. Eagly (1987) reported a meta-analysis of behavior of the two sexes in mixed groups performing joint tasks and concluded that there was a consistent tendency for men to engage in more task behavior — giving and receiving information, suggestions, and opinions — whereas women are more likely to engage in socioemotional behaviors that support positive affective relations within the group. Wood, Polek, and Aiken (1985) compared the performance of all-female and all-male groups on different tasks, finding that groups of women have more success on tasks that require discussion and negotiation, whereas male groups do better on tasks where success depends on the volume of ideas being generated. It appears that both styles are productive, though in different ways.

Although research provides insights into individual and group differences, it would be unwise to assume that all individuals and groups perform in identical ways. This caveat applies to race, ethnicity, and sexual orientation, as well as to age, gender, and SES. The school-university collaborators would do well to deal with each other as individuals. Regardless of personal beliefs, school-university collaborative partners must be willing to accord equal respect to all participants. They must be receptive to hearing from those previously denied power and access.

Communication

Effective communication is another critical consideration in making collaboration successful. Communication must be systematic. Mechanisms for formal communication should be designed. Opportunities for informal communication also should be created.

Different communication conventions, styles, and modes exist between K-12 and higher education institutions. When one adds government agencies, accrediting and professional organizations, and business partners, the communication process takes on attributes of a meeting of the United Nations. In view of this, the participants must be willing to learn the language of their partners and, if necessary, develop their own vocabulary.

Participants must be willing to engage in honest discussion about difficult issues. Differences of opinion must be expressed and settled amicably. Clear understandings may best be achieved by verbally discussing the various aspects of the collaborative venture at its outset and then recording the results of those conversations in the form of a formal document.

Collaborative Agreements. Collaborative agreements often are informal. They tend to be verbal understandings of the goals and roles of the collaborating participants. The permanence and continuance of these informal agreements depend on the understandings and commitments of the originating participants. Informal agreements are in jeopardy when those individuals leave or when their roles and relationships change. Informal agreements also are open to various interpretations by the participants as the collaboration evolves and when new participants join the initiative.

Changes in original intents and purposes are not necessarily negative factors. Collaborative agreements should be examined periodically, and new goals should be set to reflect the evolution of the process. Unfortunately, without clearly expressed and agreed-on goals, change can take the collaboration far afield of its original intents and purposes and even derail the process completely. For this reason, written agreements or memoranda of understanding are recommended.

Written agreements help the participants to articulate clearly the goals, both long-term and short-term, and to define the desired outcomes of the collaboration. In addition, written agreements should define the policies and procedures of the process, specifying the roles, rights, and responsibilities of the participants. Time-lines and milestones are useful components to include. Deciding in advance how the desired outcomes are to be determined and when the collaboration itself will be evaluated is wise. This diminishes the potential for dissatisfaction with the collaborative process and its products.

All parties participating in the collaboration should have input into the document. The document should be easily accessible at all times for reference and referral. It should be revisited periodically to see if it requires revision or alteration. Having a written agreement helps the collaboration in the long term.

The development of the document is the first collaborative act in an ongoing process. It gives the participants an opportunity to talk together and to establish the aspirations for and rules of their partnership. The tone and tenor of the initial conversations regarding the writing of the agreement are good indicators of how the collaboration itself will proceed. This is the stage in the process where trust relationships will be established.

Time

It is important to provide ample time for collaboration. The time allotted will vary, depending on goals, participants, resources, etc. Unrealistic time frames are often the cause of frustration and disappointing results in collaborative ventures. Experiments must be given sufficient time to succeed. Regression, inertia, and setbacks should be expected.

Defining the time requirements of the collaborative initiative in advance helps participants to make informed decisions about the commitment they are making and the extent to which they can wholeheartedly engage in the endeavor. It also helps them establish realistic expectations for the desired outcomes.

Collaboration is time intensive. If quick change is desired, then collaboration is not the best route to take. On the other hand, the old adage that two heads are better than one is more often true than not. Collaboration can be well worth the time if everyone shares a vision of substantive improvement based on informed deliberation and experimentation. The shared goals must be of real benefit to all partners in order to justify the time demands of collaboration.

Time is also a precious commodity for the participants. For both university and K-12 faculty, it is important that they are given release time for collaborative planning and discussion.

Resources

In addition to time, other resources are needed for effective collaboration. There must be equitable resource sharing among the partners. Long-term collaboration cannot be sustained through funding solely from grants or other short-term commitments. Collaborative partners should be realistic about what can be afforded and what can be accomplished. Commitments should not be made without careful consideration of the resources, in hand, with which to support them. Participants should not be expected to function without adequate institutional resources, nor should they be burdened with unfair demands on their own personal resources, money, or time.

It is rare for experimental projects, which is what most collaborative ventures are, to receive funds from existing organizational budgets. In education, substantial funding increases are uncommon. Increases in funding tend to keep pace with the escalating costs of existing programs and personnel. A collaborative initiative largely dependent on securing external, competitive grant funds is a high-risk venture with a limited life expectancy. Goals and timelines should be crafted with this realization.

Collaboration is a resource-intensive undertaking. Unfunded mandates to collaborate should be challenged vigorously. A lack of adequate resources seriously constrains a collaborative venture. Over the short run, sacrifices may be made willingly and gains achieved; but over the long run, inadequate resources buy inadequate results.

Roles and Responsibilities

Collaboration is highly dependent on the capabilities and dispositions of the individual participants. Specifying the roles and responsibilities of participants and their institutions can facilitate the process and enhance its outcomes. Participants should negotiate in advance to decide who does what. This reduces the likelihood of misunderstandings along the way based on varying impressions of how things were meant to be done. Clarification of roles and responsibilities reduces the risk of recrimination. It also reduces the potential for power struggles. It forces the participants to focus on the desired outcomes and the means through which the outcomes will be achieved.

Interprofessional collaboration in schools is shared decision making (Mostert 1996). Ideally, decision making should be shared equally among all participants. At the least, there must be agreement about how decisions will be made. This includes decisions about the dissolution of the collaborative initiative. The written agreement should try to outline circumstances under which the collaboration should not proceed. Conditions of termination are worth considering, discussing, and defining.

Process Assessment and Outcome Evaluation

Having defined the destination through written goals, the participants should decide what process they will use to accomplish the stated outcomes. It is wise to establish benchmarks and to designate points on the timeline when all of the participants review the process and decide whether or not to continue. This is a logical time for adjustments if the process requires them.

Performance assessment is possible if goals have been formulated in precise and measurable terms. Decisions should be made about the types of evidence that best indicate successful achievement of the stated outcomes. It is unlikely that there will be one best measure. Using multiple measures is recommended. These measures should be authentic and embedded throughout the process so that they can be used for assessment purposes along the way, as well as evaluation instruments.

It may be worthwhile to investigate traditional and nontraditional assessments in a study group so that all viable options are considered. It is wise to contact others who are engaged in similar collaborative endeavors to see what they have found useful.

A sense of accomplishment is imperative in any undertaking. The demands of collaboration are great and can take their toll on participants, especially those for whom the fruit of their labors is not apparent.

The constraining factors presented here illustrate the complex nature of collaboration. They do make collaboration seem daunting, but that is not the intent. Collaboration can be extremely rewarding. In fact, one could argue that, as social creatures, human beings are predisposed to collaborate. Collaboration is much more likely to be successful, and therefore rewarding, if it is undertaken with thoughtful consideration and planning, rather than impetuosity and naivete.

Exemplary Models

There are many successful models of school-university collaboration. Because most efforts are shaped by their participants, the models are varied. The models presented here are noteworthy because they have managed to systematize a collaborative process that deals with basic problems in exemplary and innovative ways. Contact information is provided for these projects.

Eastern Shore Association of College Presidents (ESACP). This collaborative program involves the presidents of five colleges and universities on the Eastern Shore of Maryland, including: Chesapeake College, Salisbury University, University of Maryland Eastern Shore, Washington College, and Wor-Wic Community College. The presidents and their designees work together to foster collaboration among these institutions to benefit the citizens of the region. Collaborative initiatives often include K-12 institutions, and projects have addressed such issues as the teacher shortage and professional development schools.

For more information, contact: Eastern Shore Association of College Presidents (ESACP), c/o Office of the

President, University of Maryland Eastern Shore, Princess Anne, MD 21853. Phone: (410) 651-6101.

Inter-Institutional Forum for Teacher Education (IFTE). This collaborative program involves the faculty and administrators from the departments of education at Salisbury University and the University of Maryland Eastern Shore. They work together to develop collaborative projects, share resources, and deliver educational programs in the region. They have a collaborative project in field experiences that involves the local school systems on the Delmarva Peninsula.

For more information, contact: Inter-Institutional Forum for Teacher Education, c/o Department of Education, Salisbury University, Salisbury, MD 21801. Phone: (410) 543-6280.

Or contact: Department of Education, University of Maryland Eastern Shore, Princess Anne, MD 21853. Phone: (410) 651-6217.

K-16 Partnership. This partnership of the University System of Maryland, Maryland State Department of Education, and Maryland Higher Education Commission has created opportunities for collaboration to improve school-university education and articulation.

For more information, contact: K-16 Partnership, University System of Maryland, 3300 Metzerott Rd., Adelphi, MD 20783. Phone: (301) 445-2797.

National Council of Teachers of English (NCTE) Reading Initiative. A facilitator, sanctioned by NCTE as having the requisite knowledge and expertise in the field of reading, works with a K-12 school over a two-year period in a guided inquiry process to help teachers develop greater profiency in teaching reading. Schools pay for the facilitator and the workshops provided by NCTE. Individualized goals are crafted by the participants for their own professional development, as are goals for reading program improvement.

For more information, contact: National Council of Teachers of English Reading Initiative, c/o Carol M. Jones, Project Administrator, National Council of Teachers of English, 1111 W. Kenyon Road, Urbana, IL 61801. Cjones@ncte.org. Phone: 1-800-369-6283, ext. 3627.

New Scripts for the 21st Century. Developed by researchers at the University of North Carolina at Chapel Hill, the New Scripts project is focused on creating a systems change in personnel preparation for early childhood education and intervention. Representatives of all stakeholders in the participating state come together, define areas of mutual need, prioritize needs, identify one or two to address, meet in smaller working groups with expert helpers to develop a plan with a specified timeline and outcomes, return to the larger group with their plan of action, and implement the plan. Experts are made available as consultants and outside evaluators. States engaged in New Scripts are Iowa, Kentucky, Nebraska, North Carolina, North Dakota, and Delaware.

For more information, contact: New Scripts for the 21st Century, c/o Pam Winton or Camille Catlett, University of North Carolina at Chapel Hill, Frank Porter

Graham Child Development Center, Sheryl-Mar Building, CB #8185, Chapel Hill, NC 27599. Pam Winton: pam winton@unc.edu. Phone: (919) 966-7180. Camille Catlett: camille@unc.edu. Phone: (919) 966-6635.

Professional Development School Network. This network involves faculty from the colleges, universities, and school systems in Maryland with professional development schools. They work to develop, refine, and evaluate state PDS; to plan conferences; to share resources; to provide technical assistance to higher education institutions and K-12 schools; and to disseminate information, including funding opportunities.

For more information, contact: Professional Development School Network, c/o Program Approval and Accountability Section, Ms. Maggie Madden, Program Specialist, Maryland State Department of Education, Baltimore, MD 21201. Phone: (410) 767-0564.

Statewide School-College (K-16) Partnerships. The State Higher Education Executive Officers Association supports state initiatives to create structures that more closely align K-12 and postsecondary education. They document ways various state programs support school-college collaboration and new strategies for state school-university partnerships. In addition, they have identified lessons and challenges involved in creating models for school-university systems.

For more information, contact: Statewide School-College (K-16) Partnerships, c/o State Higher Education Executive Officers, 707 Seventeenth Street, Suite 2700, Denver, CO 80202-3427. Phone: (303) 299-3685.

Conclusion

Collaboration between K-12 schools and higher education institutions is a complex undertaking. It is shaped by many forces. In addition to the differences among participants, perhaps the most critical factors that shape and sustain a school-university collaboration are the willingness to collaborate, the development of shared goals, and the creation of effective communication systems.

As the collaborative process unfolds, participants become aware of the politics and practices that characterize the institutions and individuals involved. Recognizing, respecting, and responding to these factors become critical activities for the collaborative partners.

The future holds much promise and many challenges for school-university collaboration. It represents an unprecedented opportunity to support a real and lasting change in education.

School-university collaboration will undoubtedly change in the future. Technology has and will continue to affect both the models and the means by which we collaborate. More communication will continue to take place electronically; and while this may expedite the dialogue, it will be important to recognize the importance of face-to-face communication. Clearly this is an area for research.

Collaboration between schools and universities may be the best hope for education reform. When individual and institutional differences are recognized and respected, chances for successful collaboration are increased. The benefits outweigh the barriers when interprofessional collaborators resolve to use adequate planning, a common focus, and creativity.

To paraphrase the African proverb, it takes a much larger community to educate a child, a community that involves schools, parents, and higher education. For it to be successful, the stakeholders must commit the time — time to build trust, to develop shared goals, to recognize and respect each other's unique perspectives, and to develop honest and ongoing communication. School-university collaboration is truly a work in progress, constantly evolving, and highly sensitive to the many social, political, and economic forces present in society. It is a challenging venture, but one that is here to stay.

References

Boyer, E.L. *Scholarship Reconsidered: Priorities of the Professiorate*. San Francisco: Jossey-Bass, 1990.

Cook, L., and Friend, M. "Principles for the Practice of Collaboration in Schools." *Preventing School Failure* 35, no. 4 (1991): 6-9.

DiSibio, R.A., and Gamble, R.J. "Collaboration Between Schools and Higher Education: The Key to Success." *College Student Journal* 31 (1997): 532-36.

Eagly, A.H. *Sex Differences in Social Behavior: A Social Role Interpretation*. Hillsdale, N.J.: Erlbaum, 1987.

Maccoby, E.E. "Gender and Relationships: A Developmental Account." *American Psychologist* 45 (1990): 513-20.

Maeroff, G.I. *Education and Change: A Personal Critique*. Fastback 466. Bloomington, Ind.: Phi Delta Kappa Educational Foundation, 2000.

Mostert, M.P. "Interprofessional Collaboration in Schools: Benefits and Barriers in Practice." *Preventing School Failure* 40, no. 3 (1996): 135-38.

Nnadi, E.; Cathcart, D.; Creighton, P.; and Jopp, H. "Collaboration to Cross Boundaries: University of Maryland Eastern Shore and Salisbury State University." In *Proceedings of the Annual Accreditation and Quality Assurance Conference, Middle States Association*. Philadelphia, 2000.

Pugach, M.C., and Johnson, L.J. *Collaborative Practitioners, Collaborative Schools*. Denver: Love, 1995.

Sternberg, R.J. *Making School Reform Work: A "Mineralogical" Theory of School Modifiability*. Fastback 467. Bloomington, Ind.: Phi Delta Kappa Educational Foundation, 2000.

Wise, A.E., and Lubbrand, J. "Profession-Based Accreditation." *Phi Delta Kappan* 96 (1996): 202-206.

Wood, W.; Polek, D.; and Aiken, C. "Sex Differences in Group Task Performance." *Journal of Personality and Social Psychology* 48 (1985): 63-71.

Recent Books Published by the
Phi Delta Kappa Educational Foundation

100 Classic Books About Higher Education
C. Fincher, G. Keller, E.G. Bogue, and J. Thelin
Trade paperback. $29 (PDK members, $21.75)

Whose Values? Reflections of a New England Prep School Teacher
Barbara Bernache-Baker
Cloth. $49 (PDK members, $38)
Trade paperback. $24 (PDK members, $18)

American Education in the 21st Century
Dan H. Wishnietsky
Trade paperback. $22 (PDK members, $16.50)

Readings on Leadership in Education
From the Archives of Phi Delta Kappa International
Trade paperback. $22 (PDK members, $16.50)

Profiles of Leadership in Education
Mark F. Goldberg
Trade paperback. $22 (PDK members, $16.50)

**Use Order Form on Next Page
Or Phone 1-800-766-1156**

*A processing charge is added to all orders.
Prices are subject to change without notice.*

Complete online catalog at http://www.pdkintl.org

Order Form

<table>
<tr><td colspan="4">SHIP TO:</td></tr>
<tr><td colspan="4">STREET</td></tr>
<tr><td colspan="4">CITY/STATE OR PROVINCE/ZIP OR POSTAL CODE</td></tr>
<tr><td colspan="3">DAYTIME PHONE NUMBER</td><td>PDK MEMBER ROLL NUMBER</td></tr>
</table>

QUANTITY	TITLE		PRICE

<table>
<tr>
<td rowspan="4">

ORDERS MUST INCLUDE PROCESSING CHARGE

Total Merchandise	Processing Charge
Up to $50	$5
$50.01 to $100	$10
More than $100	$10 plus 5% of total

Special shipping available upon request.
Prices subject to change without notice.
</td>
<td>SUBTOTAL</td><td></td>
</tr>
<tr><td>Indiana residents add
5% Sales Tax</td><td></td></tr>
<tr><td>PROCESSING
CHARGE</td><td></td></tr>
<tr><td>TOTAL</td><td></td></tr>
</table>

☐ Payment Enclosed (check payable to Phi Delta Kappa International)

Bill my   ☐ VISA   ☐ MasterCard   ☐ American Express   ☐ Discover

ACCT #   DATE

		/				

EXP DATE   SIGNATURE

Mail or fax your order to: Phi Delta Kappa International,
P.O. Box 789, Bloomington, IN 47402-0789. USA
Fax: (812) 339-0018. Phone: (812) 339-1156

For fastest service, phone 1-800-766-1156 and use your credit card.